Jeno Platthy

Poems of Jesus and Other Poems

For Jon

in friendship

Madrid, July 22, 1982 Jeno

POEMS
of
JESUS
and
OTHER POEMS
by
JENO PLATTHY

FEDERATION OF INTERNATIONAL POETRY ASSOCIATIONS
WASHINGTON, D.C.   ●   1982

Among other works published by the author
are the following poetry volumes:

TAVASZ 1948 Budapest
FROM BUDAPEST TO TOKYO 1957 Tokyo
SUMMER FLOWERS 1960 New York
AUTUMN DANCES 1963 Boston
TS'AU MOU 1966 Singapore & Taipei
WINTER TUNES 1974 Washington, D.C.
SPRINGTIDE 1975 Baltimore
POEMES CHOISIS 1975 Mamer
SELECCIONES DE DANZAS DE OTOÑO y FLORES DE VERANO 1975 Las Palmas
O:GALTI DIVÃLO 1980 Rajkot
COLLECTED POEMS 1981 Washington, D.C.
CHUI WU 1982 Taipei

Copyright © 1982 by Jeno Platthy
Manufactured and printed in the United States of America
Library of Congress Catalog Card Number: 82-082541

ISBN 92-9042-002-2

First edition. First printing.
Published for the occasion of the VIth International Congress of Poets, Madrid

C O N T E N T S

PART ONE

POEMS OF JESUS

PART TWO

OTHER POEMS

P A R T O N E

P O E M S O F J E S U S

"... those who have become so mean that one would
think Jesus Christ wasted his time to die on the Cross
for that kind of men."

                 Carol Louise Abell: November's Nemesis
                      from her FIVE LEAF CLOVER (1982)

"The stone the angel rolled away with tears
Is back upon your mouth these thousand years."

                 Edna St.Vincent Millay: To Jesus on His Birthday
                      from her THE BUCK IN THE SNOW (1928)

I

Beyond the open and formlessness many
faint recognitions of puppet shows and
theaters occur. In front of the eye of
soul images march. The meaning does not
come into view. Struggling is more
marked. Theories created by scholars
which, astonishingly, fit old works of art,
in the beyond cannot be applied. Life is
so abrupt one cannot waste even a second
of it. Surprises awaiting on the other side
meet most everybody unprepared.
Absence of landscape.
And we go, all, into a land without
topographic features, with the hope
that there is, somewhere, an end.

II

I not only know whence have we come but
also to where we all will go. In these
great wanderings the subtlest part of
man trying life beyond this earthly one
dwells mostly not within but above.
Seeing the world lovely, saying things
complimentary about contemporaries, singing
odes to an occasion or a person, was never
an honor for a poet but always a duty.
Suffering through one's soul affects fate
and future. Echoes of the wordless word
from the heart of meek, innocent and good
prompt strong men to pray.

                        To towns where
pelargoniums hang in straw baskets and
roses set in motion by the wind are run,
I will come back after the judgment, -
a pink umbrella against the dark, the sun.

III

Heaven is an empire where your thoughts take you,
where you meet your dreams. It is hard to detect
the air's waves but more hard to observe the
waves of love. Super-sensitive hearts trace
our origin as we come from the eternal beyond
where objects, images are viewed as ourselves.
What is above is not the same anymore as below
and what is below is different vastly from the
things above. Before and after have no
meanings; doom and glory are the same. Desires
drag down the heart: don't wait patiently
for the end of the world to come.
Inimitable color of flowers in a mirror: over
the brocade horizon in the sumptuous silence
one sees only the setting sun and the sea.

IV

I talked to the stars and learned that dreams
go very far, even beyond them. With words
not spoken by lips I talked to the void,
commanding the visible to come out of it.
We know not who are we or what is life, only
that we are part of a whole. Basic character
built in several life-times cannot be erased
during one here. How strongly a single
event is tied to a meaningful new arrangement
of stars! Images in a dream: non-stop experiences.
We guess who is behind the flashing happenings
of the inner eye. Unceasing croaking of frogs
in summer, falsetto quarrel of migrating crows:
the nearer one gets to death the more interested
he will be in the journey of the soul.
I see the stars bleeding.

V

Deservedly black future.
In bad business offices signs say:
"Take a number and wait." We wait in life.
Baseness and callousness of human nature
prevail and spoil the best of minds and hearts.

Earth is peopled by persons of the underground.
Days full of cussedness.
Enfeoffed by cunning violence,
fierce, futile fib and feint.
Poets with quiet asperity tell what
others did not see: long necked flowers
swimming out of a garden as swans.
A pair of yellowhammers.
Rapt in plum-hued blush of dreams
one is too wise to write.

Claimant for the highest honors,
having a gift for clean dreams, in the
dusk I see her and all the girls crying.
Her soul in unison with other souls, puts
the tear-drops up in the sky, one by one,
to shine as stars forever, decorating
the universe for our own time.

VI

They say when God was crying and his tears
fell on the universe the world became his
countenance, the breath of his the souls.
He was crying because of solitariness. Fighting
against himself, against his own thoughts,
feelings and will. And the souls condensed,
merged with matter, became alive with great
carelessness. As men they are occupied in
producing time. But nothing great or immortal
happens in finite time. Neither marble nor
gilded monuments of bronze will outlive the
power of verse. From the meadow of verbs, from
the river of rhymes, mountain of metaphors,
listen to the trumpet of daffodils, the hosannas
sang by the throats of lilies and lips of
trilliums. Time is an appendage, extension
of the soul. And this is the increase of it.
Leave aside the earth then or time
takes away whatever you earned.

VII

When the earth was destroyed in fire
all life was extinguished on it.
One cannot make a mistake, putting
too much importance on things of earth.
There is different time in each soul and
we live in time and yet we don't live in it.
Dreams are above it. Ferocious rushes,
blind changes, intemperate happenings.
I collect my tears in a black-figured vase.
Written upon the hearts: in eternity
yellow and blue roses unceasingly bloom.
Solidified time.
Once everything comes to an end.
And as you pluck flowers, the
wind of God will take you then away.

VIII

Poetry is the sound uttered in spite of
being alive. Knowing and being are not the same.
An object, idea has no knowledge of its being
but still exists. If nothing exists then
everything does not cover nothing: these are
mutually exclusive concepts. Today philosophers
can neither formulate new and proper questions
nor grasp the originality and depth of old ones.
The cosmos is too complex, too vast for
understanding through human speech: we are still
at an embryonic state of artistic expression.
Beyond comprehension the meaning and magnitude
of the presented reality. Psychic forces
penetrating the universe might be confined to a
small part of it: we are not getting impulses,
messages, recollections of different worlds and
galaxies. Divine is man's own nature. Poetry
is his cry. The yellow roses offer their
incomparable gold and in the rose-red city the
lilacs wave their mauve lanterns in the wind.

Life is a long, arduous race to the finish.
Few realize that it is better to hurry.
One feels pressures of the blood to do
other things in life, not the dutiful ones.
When peace of life is taken away or unknown,
it's concealed that birth is a beginning of
a chance. Seeing a soul departing we remain
speechless for long, dragging the dawns
on a string. Diluted times: tempi
of crickets in the languishing fall drawn
out for long intervals. And in these rigid
times if there are words commensurate with
great thoughts, they speak as it were of
two different things, the Only and the One.

X

I should be fain to regard this topsey-turveydom
of world, unfitting pretenses as beyond which there
is an empire. Thoughts take you there and you meet
your dreams. Apparently much happens between death
and birth about which only art is competent to
form an opinion, illustrating the idea of
transformation. How one can appear as someone else
and change back. Our entire appearance on earth
is an illustration of this transformation.
We may have a number of roles. We were someone
else while we were ourselves. The more noisy
pace of days the hectic rush it brings, the
more our yearning for simple things appears,
in the rustling of the eucalyptus trees and
the gentle moving of the autumn-flaming figs.

Altered space and time illustrate the
spaciousness of spirit, bitterness of life.
Circumcised lips sing the glory and praise
of impenetrable heaven: my exiled soul is
waiting there to land. When I was young
I was kneading pigeons, swallows and
sparrows out of clay and made them fly
with a hiss. Now in the golden crown
of blaze the royal sun reminds us,
even the one who longs to forget, but
cannot, the torture of years. Harvesting
roses, the blue roses of the sea in a
net as rings around the sun crown of
clouds gathers above in a flame-wreath:
the harpist autumn rips the reddish woods
of pomp recalling the songs of a childhood:
"I did not want such horses, Mother,
the green horses of war!"

XII

If we would keep our memories when returning
from death, mankind would improve vastly and
there wouldn't be crime. We would remember horrors,
accidents and tragedies, deeply engraved in the
soul but also embraces, kisses and love. Angels
supply lines to this poem and sing in unison an
old hymn not heard in recent times: "You are the
sugar of the world." The crimson fabric of dreams
covers the tattered garment of pride: looking down
on hordes of men as ants. In the golden robe of
autumn the ship of the sun sails the tumultuary, the
flutist wind practices bravura solos. Oh grant me
that I may not question why I'm on earth, my Lord.

XIII

Long distance runners of faraway lands
who are concerned only with their missions
and are in flight for days on end:
we are such persons. The way of truth is
a divided highway with many lanes but
we encounter, never, a soul. We wonder,
rightly, how can one be born twice to the
same mother or how can the infinite grace
of the Father grant between two eternities
that we will return the same honors to the
same persons again? There are no windows
on the hearts so desires cannot be seen,
but the eyes are windows to reveal the
hearts. Modesty, more precious than
diamonds. Live with a quiet heart, with
bronze guts, without deceit. Don't be
handcuffed to the present. Think of future
and go through the dreams from the
dark, blood-colored dusk of spring.

XIV

City of Dreams in the *Odyssey* refers to
a well known place which does indeed exist,
where bodiless intelligences work constant
on future and present. City of Dreams.
Blue sun in the green sky.

Few take the trouble to get oriented
with the origin of the soul, the hows of our
journey to earth and the ways of being.
The chosen ties of relations are given up
with plunging into the pleasures of life.
The soul's absolute certainty gives way to
the haziness and slick trenchancy of logic.
But still, life must be worth living, since
so many are willing to die for freedom
in the unseen presence of the Lord.

How can we say more than our gestures,
smiles and eyes say, portray and suggest?
How can we say more than our words imply?
Words slip out and shock with their truths.
Words are swords. Only the best of books
deal with the soul. It's important for man
to feel the skies above and his relations
around. But how can we say more than the shapes
of flowers say and their fragrances? How can
we say more than the songs of birds and the
geometric pattern of flapping butterfly wings?
More than the whispers of pines in the breeze
and the red blooming poppy fields merging
with the wine-colored sunset of the sky?

XVI

The afterlife of man is depersonalized,
scary and has nothing to do with earth.
They say there are as many stars in the skies
as souls on earth. But how individual souls
depart from the Lord and how they return
to the eternal light is not communicated.
How a light fuses with an invisible one, -
even poets can't explain. Life is such a
side-issue of existence that it is better left
unspoken and untouched. Incidentality of life
doesn't reach the soul. Laws of the heavenly
existence override concerns: the material
universe in its temporariness and the
immaterial one in its unsuspected splendour.

XVII

Not only what comes out of your mouth
defiles you: your thoughts equally
contaminate. Cease to think them. Cease
to use your tongue when it's not blessing.
Heart, source of some evilish things: do
not use it if it does not lift you above
the ways of earth. Blessed are who have
been persecuted in the hearts and the ones
who were before they came into existence.
We all will take up stones and fight
for I have not come to throw peace upon
the world. Afflicted soul: see the
trees of Paradise which neither wither
in autumn nor bloom in the spring.
If you can guess the beginning, you
already know most about the end.

XVIII

Resurrection is the promise that you will
come back again and again, although you might
not remember why and for whose glory.
Resurrection is to know that your soul
separates from the body. Resurrection is
to know that life is greater than death.
Laws are in the hearts. We flee
nowhere and when going forward remain
in the same spot. Let your heart not grind
on worries and let your spirit not be worn
by constant troubles of the world.
Prepare yourself for life while here.
Praise is one of the ingredients of life.

Beings from above, the illuminated ones,
made entirely of light, in moral cloaks, to help.
Be wise in the heart: return to yourself.
Death is a library where you are shelved until
someone uses, reads and needs you again.
It beseems me, who have been in the rest,
to say nothing more at this time.

XIX

Stay away from those who are polite out of
cunning. From those who put on the garb of
decency to deceive. From those who masquerade
under false pretenses and use a position to harm.
Run away from those who have second thoughts.
Run away from cheats, liars, the double-hearted,
the mealy-mouthed and from those neither male
nor female but called 'it', the itsters. Run
away from the world. It is full of crooks,
educated bums, moral hooligans, seducing teachers.
Turn your back on them and spit on their words.
Honesty is a mask under which they commit
heinous crimes. The most wicked ones are
those who pretend to be good.

Man creates God to his own likeness as
once God created man to his. Heaven is
the spirit and according to oral
tradition of the baptized, learning
must exist in the soul first to know
the affairs of God. Earth is a temple
and we are all one with another.
Newborns amazed at the newness of
identity, who they are.
We are visited while in another form.
Who wears clothes within?
Gift of goodness, large destiny looms
ahead of us according to birth.
We know we are and are not of this world.
Receiving the glory we reap the entire crop
of life. Tresses of marble lilacs
and never tarnished gold where the
fragrance of rosemary and wild sage is
mixed by the breeze along the seashore...

XXI

I am the silence and the thunder,
I am the peace and I am the war.
I am poverty and wealth asunder,
I am the portal and I am the bar.

I am the hate and I am the goodness,
I am the seasons, time and pride.
I am the bread, I am the wine-press,
I am the bridegroom and the bride.

I am the mother of my father,
I am the future and what was before.
I am the blessed and the cadaver,
I am the heaven and I am the door.

XXII

I am singing praises of slanderers,
those full of hatred with no cause.
I am singing praises of captives of greed
who steal and kill and maim.
In thoughts they know me not and since the
thoughts of the heart are alien to them,
I praise them in showing the power of words.
We live among the most cursed, dishonoured,
wanton and impious ones, among those who deal
in bodies and fallen into bestiality,
attached to fraudulence, corrupt desires, - .
That these might not be condemned forever to hell
and thus renounce evesdropping, blasphemy, sloth,
belly-love, play-acting and pitilessness.
In these difficult times I sing their praises
in songs composed in the heart.
I was writing with finger in the sand and
also writing thoughts on water. But these
poems are not written with black ink on white
paper but carved on red granite with an axe.

XXIII

Upon the completion of time and space
the end will come down on all. Abolishing
the age when rampant wickedness mounts to
the skies, the firmaments will fall, the
rivers stop flowing and planets rotate.
Everybody will die. Signs performed.
Chastized out of the cosmos, the walls of
darkness will fall upon us, crumbling
and burying all for good. The mind is
a treasure, the body is a rose.
God passes through the heart and sets it
shining, without one's knowing. He sweeps
down on the tired and in shortened times
gives them strength, halos on the pates.
At the boundaries of ways we will come back
from invisibility, souls will appear again
in quickened rows, anew, made out of
perspiration, tears and breath of God, and
man will no longer be a dream of a shadow.

XXIV

Light-land of the skies reflects the greatness
and exultance of the ascending universe,
the invisible light-robe of the envied
and the flood-lit City of Light.
Universe is a black hole, heaven the
light, the freedom and the life.
Sun-immersed glory of the clean ones.
Birds of heaven sing in silence, sons of
dreams sing the odes of One who cannot
be spoken to. Songs of light, about the
power to become invisible, about the
iridescent trees of an eternal spring.
Realm of light, the great uncontainable.
Light behind the sun, overshadowing it
in brightness and deluding it with
glory, dazzling hope and faith so shining
that the world is still in its shadow.

XXV

Plowshares plow a poem into the soil, a
furrow at a time, as farmers express
themselves. Blacksmiths beat it out on
an anvil with hammers as red-hot ornament.
Drivers drive a metrical pattern so,
weavers weave a thread on the loom.
Tailors stitch and loop it out.
Unique lines are written by gestures,
by smiles, embraces and by tears.
Mothers write the most beautiful ones
with concern, attention, love and care.
Cleaners clean the meaning of an old,
forgotten phrase and teachers teach
hearts to throb, eyes to shine.
Cooks distill the aroma of poems,
and actors play verses on a stage.
Mailmen often deliver a comma, an
exclamation mark, in an envelope.
One who does not work with his hands
sighs a poem with every breath.
Poems are what machines and robots do not
accept and cannot produce. Poetry is
missing from the hectic rush of life.
Poems are when you stop to think and work for
an hour or decide to be friendly for a day.
When you have no reason at all but still
think it is the time to celebrate the
power of words as charms.
I was nailed to the cross with long spikes
but you are nailed with pain and worry,
with problems to your every day.

XXVI

They may question how I know what I do know
and from where I obtained my knowledge. Once,
when young, coming home from the vineyards,
I met one in a light-robe. My mother tied her
to a bed. We recognized each other at once, she
was my look-alike, my second self. We merged.
And from that moment I had access to our Father
in heaven. I do not know how many may have merged
with their overselves or with that part of soul
which is above, joining in dangers and in dreams.
From then I instantly knew and realized
thoughts, problems of others, how to heal and
bless them. In the grip of God I can move
mountains. This gift is limited by the universe
and the Father whom we call the Lord. Our earthly
stay stands in a reverse manner to the budding,
part-blooming apricot branches as they claw
against the threatening, dark-gray sky.

XXVII

What eyes cannot measure in its endless roving,
I'll be the seas and will fill the valleys.
I'll be the fire which consumes the globe,
I'll be the mountain to cover all the lands.
I'll be the air and dry up the earth. If
one starts anywhere near himself, he reaches
the end and at the end meets God. The whole
world is a path to walk on, where the left
road, the right road and no road are one.
The rivers talk, forests fume, the winds warn:
Armageddon is a place, try to avoid it.
Read and interpret the signs.
Simonides speaks of the demon of tomorrow and
I speak about future, crushing down on us.

XXVIII

I have overcome the world, the vast
community of thiefs, robbers, murderers
and intimidated ones. I have overcome
myself above the vinyards shepherding
black goats while the hoary head
of autumn mountains looked down on
ling, harebell and white henna fields.
Overcoming births lives can be saved.
Fortress is the heart.
What I say still cannot be understood.
Regardless of talent and background
one comes to earth with, he is doomed
to failure from the start.
The expectant world lives in sinful
ignorance about keeping God constant in
mind, about humility, the refusal of
wealth and about silence which we fight
against with swords.

XXIX

My hunger is my cook and my thirst is
my refreshment. The cloven skies of the
besieged heaven will remain open.
Stones turn to bread in the clear,
invisible air. Never touching the earth
while going, I walk on the sea and command
the storms to cease. But those who cannot
believe in miracles do not believe in me
either. I am not the one whom you see and
I show myself for someone else who does
not have an eye. The ugly see themselves
in me and the good fear me when I look.
I brought the light with me to earth and
my message is about the end coming red-hot.
I say to you if you live for me a little,
I will die for you a lot.

XXX

In your need I was always with you
and in my thoughts you never ran away.
I am alone but you are with me constant.
I command mountain-peaks to sing and
speak and I train the ears to hear
a never-ending song. Heaven is most
everywhere where you are and we
are to help God in his work. We have
to learn to live in both worlds.
Silence is a strong wall, hard to tear
it down. But days will come when the sun
will not rise, when mornings will not
greet you anymore. Who does not have his
cross is no friend and I say to you: turn
your back on the world and follow me to live.

XXXI

I am the truth and I am the falsehood,
I am the darkness and I am the lamp.
I am the hunter and I am the pursued,
I am the wolf and I am the lamb.

I am the plan and I am the building,
I am the quiet and who does disturb.
I am the law and the unyielding,
I am the action and I am the word.

I am the marble and I am the plaster,
I am the child and who gives support.
I am the servant and I am the master,
I am the last one and I am the Lord.

XXXII

You can be killed, mugged, raped and probably
you will be because lawlessness is great.
You can be maimed, paralyzed and crippled
in involving yourself to save someone else.
Our roads are not safe, neither is the home:
no one can assure your sleep or that you
will bring up a child in decency and peace.
Lawmakers, judges, police are the guilty.
Corrupting influence of what you hear and read,
messages that override the words of the cross; -
take the laws into your own hands and I say,
promise that God will absolve you from wrong.
As on the lowlands one can see nothing but
the sky, not even far off in the vastness
the faint outlines of lavender mountains:
where was our origin? My coming to earth
starts a moral revolution and a social purge.
I often said that if someone throws stones at
you, take up and throw bread back at him. But
if I would know that two thousand years hence
the world would still be as crime-infested,
vicious and false as today, I would ask the
Father to destroy it in a blast of flame.

XXXIII

Opposite of this life is heaven where you
are on your own and do not bully, exploit
others and cannot commit crimes.
You face yourself in the inmost sense and
the rampage of life, where many punished
for sins of others, exists only in traces.
You are much above life and see clear that on
earth where mankind could and should have
been much better, we neglect ourselves
to a high degree. The fury of masses would
kill not only the son of, but also, God,
himself, were he close in a visible form.
The rottenness of spirit and the foul-smell
of souls makes me impatient with the works
of nature even with the blessed rain that
falls on the region once or twice a year.

XXXIV

What a destiny it is to die in the spring
when nature comes alive with the promise
of flowers and the prospects of a year!
Not all sins and crimes can be atoned in
advance and not even I can assume the
burden of guilt for not-yet happened crimes.
Drinking flames and fire as God-possessed,
speaking unstoppable day and night the Voice,
the last hour of the race is upon us, the
gates are closed and the judgment has began!
Be honored those who receive visions and who
have crystal tongues and still remain mute.
One has thrown some cut flowers here and
there on the table for a last supper.

XXXV

Ah, to be so indignant, upset and enraged
over the mistreatment of people that one
can't ever smile, relax or unwind!
Horrifying is to look at life.
Abominable misery. Beating the breasts in
rhythm the fearless. Hopelessness and
shock huddles the poor. Creatures, rejected,
envy the dogs and wild beasts, pray
for liberation from the world.
Repugnancy of lives. Never was earth
meant to live on and the after-life
of heaven is no consolation, not an
incentive to pull through the years.
Angels with insides turned out, having
no outsides, in temper tantrums
dole the vendetta out of balance.
Madness of the tongue, wailing, frothy
lips, growling under the steel eyes:
silence the answer.
The red sunset of a balm spring day
harangues the bloodshed of the end.

XXXVI

Cleansed by prayers when one's praying all night
to know the will of God and to act with it:
clean souls regain and collect a tiny scrap of
that subtle essence which radiates from above.
Prayers reach the land that even dreams cannot.
Heavens help, lift, elevate those who can
communicate in the gentlest terms with them.
Prayers are the roses of the spirit, the
means to reach beyond ourselves. The rustled
warmish breeze and the fast-moving foamy clouds
announce spring. The trees are all white, pink
or red with flowers, without yet the leaves.
The spring of mankind and now it is its fall.

XXXVII

Pity those who do not dream, can't remember
and do not cry on being born on earth.
Pity those who wear a mask over their hearts.
Pitiful it is that you can neither live
nor die here or in any other land.
Seeing a voice in colors but hearing it not,
seeing dreams around but cannot pick them up,
rocks, glowing in red seraphic fire:
we must be immersed more deep to see.
Between overdue springs and advance harvests,
poetry is a soul's brilliance. It is the
testimony of those who're weary of the world
and try to break out of it with imagination,
faithful inner life, spirit. Who write lyric
poems in a tragic age ought to be admired.
They see something through a heavy veil.
Poetry, not written by hand.

XXXVIII

Few are on speaking terms with God, the
magnitude of glory is too great to grasp.
Few people know his address or even his name,
and few call on him, his number is secret.
It's hard to dip inside, to bend so low as
to feel the circumference of God's grace.
Criminals carry wickedness to extreme
but since the earth has been created
no one carried goodness to excess.
Love, not of the body but of the soul and
mind that transcends existence, and peace
of the hearts which speaks aloud as wails of
the rabble or on the day of wrath the cries
of stones which in silence we still hear:
these I bring. In my Father's name they cheat
and use him as a tool to defraud, shortchange.
In spite of all things in the sunset
waves wash the sky over the endless sea.

XXXIX

If one can create the greatest silence
around him in the most hectic and turbulent
age of man, surely he can create a great
noise about him after he is gone.
Are you not victims of envy that you
cannot see although you have eyes?
Are you not slaves of hate that you
cannot hear although you have ears?
Are you not crippled by a distrust that you
cannot love although you have hearts?
Are you not obsessed by a passion that you
cannot follow me although you have reason?
Cast your anger into the sea or it'll burn
you up. On the tree of fire flowers of flame.
But why should one count the leaves of trees and
why should one count the number of spokes of
the setting sun? Lives continue with many
beginnings. You all walk as in a slumber, it
seems, but in you I and the Father are one.

XL

Miracles move the faithless and the fearful
but mean very little to those who believe.
Turning to the power which is at the bottom
of each soul requires faith. Gaining God's
approval and his consent suggests to know him.
Forgiving past sins corrects defects.
Re-thinking the commandments I give you a
new one: give twice as much love as you receive.
Live your life cleaner. Walking on the lake
in the dead of night frightens small souls
but fortifies the strong. Before long
you all will see miracles: the stars and
sun descending and returning to their
heavenly places again and again.

XXXXI

I never really thought I belong to this world,
for this world is not mine. It is not
peaceful or conducive to live in. Here most
men are fugitives from a heavenly justice,
sent to earth to finish a term. The most
despicable gathered in one place. Horrors
of life reflect the horrors of men. Cleavage
between our origin and this life. I am from
another world that often cancels this one.
It is time that man grows out of this world
and harvests his hopes in the heavenly home.
Ruddy flare of torches from the other shore
indicates they await us over there. The moon
is framed by an outer-circle, the stars set
in lighted square boxes and the emptiness
moves the gold-lavender flowers of the sun.

XXXXII

Take up your cross and follow me, I say, and
care for the glory that doesn't shine on earth.
Take up your burden and be a David against
Goliath odds and against the tides.
No one is lost who still can be helped and
all can be helped who have not perished.
Honesty is not taught in any school on earth
and few put loyalty to God above monetary gains.
No one fears the righteous for there is none
and no one respects the wise or the truthful
because there is a shortage of them today.
Cast your eyes upon the skies and see the
new signs and the new hope which is given all,
over the rushing time, the love of song,
the gift of God, that unsurpassable
glory that doesn't shine on earth.

XXXXIII

Birth-pangs of the new age have already begun:
the world reels with discord from side to side.
A new era of mankind I am announcing, new
men to come with a new Adam. We see a
cataclysm which brings about the change
and harbingers future. I look at it with
an open eye and look back at the past with
an eye-witness freedom. Deeper than the hearts,
into the soul, the happenings. Look, the clouds
over the matted hills with the fronded palms
in the air describe the visible scent of white
roses from distant Greek islands, heavy.
It is time to make the holy places once again
holy and the heart of man once again pure.

XXXXIV

I am the cold and I am the burning,
I am the morning and I am the night.
I am the content and I am the yearning,
I am the darkness and I am the light.

I am the chain and I am the freedom,
I am the mute and I am who speaks.
I am the grant and the petition,
I am the one lost and I am who seeks.

I am the mended and I am the rift,
I am the whole and I am the part.
I am the levy and I am the gift,
I am the blessing and I am the heart.

I am the glory and I am the scandal.
I am the scythe and I am the hay.
I am the foot and I am the sandal,
I am the forest and I am the way.

The shuddering poor regard those who are not
as hopeless as they as angels and with blessings
they retaliate. They are reborn and reborn
daily. Turning tragedies into miserable joys
they see God almost everywhere. There is no
greater wish in them that all should see and
hear God, that he may reveal himself to all...
Living at the outer limit of his endurance, they
do not have a leverage to deal with anyone,
even less with themselves. Not being taught
business or the trickery of merchants, - they
don't need to be told what it means to be poor.
They look at others as a fragrance at basalt,
unapproachable hard, unbendable, rigid.
If it does not renew human heart, it is
a false season the spring which renews
the earth so many a time during a life.
Pages written on human hearts in haste
they see in every passersby the reflected
splendour from the unseen face of God.

IIIIL

Children are the closest in resemblance
to the soul of man, appearance of God.
Children are in whom knowledge has not yet
manifested its destructive force.
Children are still in the Paradise of Eden
where we all were before chasen out by sword.
We are part of God, so behave according
to his holiness and sanctity of the place.
Children give measure of man's greatness.
They have no inkling of time or future,
remorse of past or fear of destiny.
Most illnesses derive from sadness.
From the dark cedar forest a dove descends
slow to the roof of the white adobe hut.
Fillets tie the elderberries to the fence.
The merciless sun heats the landscape and
the nearness of God vibrates the heart.

IIIL

I cannot stop my enemies from killing me
and force them to accept my words as true.
I cannot change, even with God's help,
the thinking of those who worship money
and frolic in the temporariness of flesh.
I only know that my hour has not come,
yet it will. Escape it I cannot. I cannot
accept that for a few years' or but for a
few days' advantage over others, people
abandon principles and the security of
an eternal life after death. I cannot
stop being God's spokesman and possess
him as I am owned by him within. The spring's
bloom is an unstoppable one: praising giant
blue flowers of the sky, the almost
invisible gold flowers of the soul and
the translucent red flowers of the heart.

IIL

Things which are to come shall be shaped differently
from expected appearance of events on earth.
Things which cannot be seen are in a storehouse
for mankind and appear sometimes as shadows on
the world. Annointed with sacredness and good heart,
declining the frenzy of the eyes, speaking in
tongues, shaking as well as dancing, the circumcised
minds prepare for the Lord. You all will be
crucified with me and wafted up to God.
Fragile pottery is man, seamed on all sides.
Light that envelopes all, radiates from bulbs,
buds, petals of flowers and leaves of trees, the
unceasing beauty of the world. A river of light
flows with fulgent fire, efflorescing flashes of
hues, the gleaming sparks. Man is part of this
new heaven, glory and splendour. And be it so.

PART TWO

OTHER POEMS

DEATH OF EROS

Tears falling inwards. Shock.
The world does not want to realize
Eros is dead.
We search for love. Mimic it.
Yearning for decency of art, moral
herosim, greatness of soul, an outward
sign of nobleness, courage: we sink
into complacency, fear, hedonism.

Mankind is too big a nation, even our
country is too big as a unit. Those who
crave for equality and rights, never speak
of rights of others or loving of enemies...
We believe in life after death but our
adversaries believe in nothing.

Old initiation of girls, winged melodies
of girl-choruses about Eros,
brilliance of late autumn afternoons
when sun lit the reddening trees aflame...

Crimes more hideous than nightmares in hell:
the atrociousness of hate, vicious, vile persons.
An Oriental painting, almost empty:
in the corner of your life a poem.

MYCENAEAN DINNER

Timelessness of Delos where beginning and end
of life does not exist and expectant mothers
are ferried quickly away along with those
nearing the end. The open sky collapses

in a summer shower while we travel to hear
Dodona's sacred gabbling, scaring some
from this common empire of the wakeful to
individual worlds of dreams, the dead.

No, this is Mycenae. Sun flogs the landscape.
Girls gather samphire below the bay trees,
narcissi bloom and spathe of black arum lily.
The sheep wander in twos and threes. Wind whips

the wiry grass, shakes the light across the gulf
where boats anchored in the sky's reflection.
Time goess in the flickering scarlet wood-fire,
among fennels, celeries and figs. Lambs roasted,

sprinkled with wine. Barley cooked in cauldrons.
Ribbed roses: time leaves a pathway, traces
of doings among the wavering walls of stone.
Wherever time goes I will go with you.

L E O N A R D O   D A   V I N C I

High above the sea, between two pillars of a
ruined temple, one watches a boat. The landscape
freezes into topaz with the dusk and across
the sea, among myriads of broken mirror-pieces,
a golden carpet leads to the low lying sun.
Victory disguised as a disaster. We know more
nowadays but understand less. Most of mankind
is evil. Tossing the details of an altar-fresco:
girls in white robes, wearing tinsel-sashes and
silver wreaths in hair, descend a staircase,
carrying lighted candles on their heads and also
in hands. The middle one wears a red sash and
golden crown with spires of lighted tapers. Acapella
singing. Of yellow ribbons the evening sky is full.

RAVENNA

Eternity is depicted with artistry that
surprises the soul. Rainbow shadings of persons
and animals document an age when emphasis was
on the morally beautiful and poverty was
tied to spiritual and moral ugliness.

Lyre-guillotine. Ivy woven around heart-shaped
leaves. Ocean border limits the movements.
As the sun comes up dew-drops in the
small florets reflect tiny stars.

Eyes of peacocks' tails watch meandering
tourists whispering: "Why did Aeschines oppose
that Demosthenes be rewarded with a golden crown
for his virtue, uprightness and services to the
people and why Demosthenes did not propose that
Aeschines be also crowned? Or his own crown be
given to him? Why do we not honor outstanding
individuals?" One ties a knot from rainbow in his
thoughts and hears crickets in mid-November nights.

T E L E M A N N

Coming to live on earth from another planet
in shining armor and with a strange weapon,
our chief concern was to avoid and disarm a
Roman soldier and then to taste vegetables
in the garden whether they will sustain us...
Life on earth, from which after many centuries
still not able to disintricate ourselves,
started with fear. Tufa walls of life around.
Warrened in individual lives as in a stone
heaven, hooked by love. From the hovering neums
and quarter tones we yearn for the unsyncopated
dance of breeze, for rainbows arranged in geometric
patterns and the golden garments of gods approving
intellectual thews, the primacy of esteem...

NOT NEED TO GO FAR

Not need to go far, the end is near and
the last day of the world is always
the end of one's own life. A raiment
we wear God instead of sins.

Distilling poetry out of tragedies and
subhuman characters to prove that there
is no more holy than life and
God is that mental fire

which keeps the world rolling. Singing
superb songs in praise of some
difficult moments wrestled out of years.
Consolation is to know

someone who has the most beautiful
dreams the world had ever known
and all the dreams are wrapped
in gold, in stars, in love...

AUTUMN   LEAVES

Sense of heroism and sense of fate embrace
one who has no choice. Quickens the pace.
Sporting with human follies
as each chiseled down with an invisible blow:
the yellow-browngold leaves fall like snow.

Invasion of visions: beings blast out
of a furnace and in the air float about,
- harebells, fangs and thongs.
God-smith who imagines him to sow,
the yellow-browngold leaves fall like snow.

Continuous weeping furrows the cheeks.
Humming tide of overmighty grief speaks,
cries without language.
Each leaf with its tremendous sorrow:
the yellow-browngold leaves fall like snow.

New collections of knowledge intervene:
the beauty of nature that we have seen
as such will last
because we have known it and said it so.
The yellow-browngold leaves fall like snow.

D E R A I L M E N T S   II

Magistraight

voluntears

jawsling

kneedom

conkisstadors

pianomise

purplendicular

peeple

mashmerized

sombrerosed

lapellent

aurora morealis

Nie Gelungen Lied

freeling

mentholity

belltions

infantory

slikorice

harp-attack

rainbowl

thirteenly

nasturtiumized

beastlification

guided muscletoe

wordtuary

sillicosis

eggcelent

flagsible

insected

leobard

rhapsadist

bathketball

puffler

hodge-fudge

albatrosis

topistry

sherriers

cramberry

Jenocide

CURRENT AFFAIRS

It was always so
that man was yearning for peace
and quiet and found only wars.
In the surplice of clouds
not the sun and glory but roars
of war-machines, missiles.
Longhand writings of waves on
sandy beaches describe destruction.
Synthetic barbarism: industrial
belching, contaminated skies.
Armed with poetry we hope still
to win the soul against odds.
Hooligans, jerks in guise of prophets,
priests. Mechanically subordinated society
in a transitional state, cursed, for
not paying enough attention to dreams,
overlooking the blunders of leaders.
The horizon is closing on us.
New generations come, more adventurous,
careless, burying science, society, art,
achievements of civilization.
Moral beggars. Torturing with dreams.
Degas' undated letter to Monet about a new
preface to Mallarmé's poems which he
'cannot understand!
Lively discussion on the topic of boring.
Only those who were and are poor
know the precise distinction between
nothing, zero, nil and ziltch.

RAOUL WALLENBERG

Towering above the century the supergiant statue
of a Swede whose life and deeds crown history.
When time was sorest, darkest, he came.
It takes not much prophesying to say his
invisible statue will soon be cast in bronze.

Life is a string of set-backs, failures, due mainly
to wickedness of others. No matter how often it is
repeated, man is slow to perceive the advantages of
a clean life. Hero who did not publicize his deeds,
his supreme devotion to a just cause: he was confident
to help beyond himself. No currency or gold can measure
goodness. As his example requires, words hardly reach
him. Above words are realms, happenings, objects and
facts with significance for human life, for future.
Beyond description are things we must contend with.
Divine origin of man never disputed: Phoenix is man.
The oneness of life misleads many. We all undergo
successive births and deaths, deprived of memory to
recall. But when one's greatness grows into the ages
and harvest of his goodness storms the skies: was he
showing how one stays clean in a tempest of filth?
Distributing pardons in the face of death, saving
lives, living sunbeam was he, personified hope.

When a tyranny is overthrown, a new dictatorship
proves it is more vicious, oppressive and hellish
than the vanquished. Filled with God's power,
invincible force, without hesitation and regard for
risks, he flung himself in the face of danger and fate.

Injustice always cries loud. The one who should be
singled out, decorated and glorified for his services
to mankind, by a terror was thrown to jail. He did
immortal favours for all of us. What did he care for
fame! What did he care for praise, thanks, honor! That
blazing courage and unselfishness reflect his nation's
scale and prompt me to say I am not worried about the
future of the world. Greater the danger, stronger the
determination to face it. As years go by, clearer his actions
become, his greatness more obvious and deeper his humanity.
Heroism does not come from reasonableness or logical
sympathy but from the very bottom of the heart. It is for this
that he was whisked away from Budapest, in order not to let
Soviet heroism be overshadowed by his triumphs and personal
magnetism. His fame rests not on the indictment of the age
but on grateful honor and esteem of the saved and on the
regard of the diplomatic communities of various nations
whose duties and missions were by him so nobly symbolized.

Our age is great because he was with us and
our age is great because we can sing of him.
We have enough circumstantial evidence to point
accusing fingers to the East of Sweden and to
point our grieving hearts to tyrants of the East.
How does one face terror, torture and wickedness
when he is outstandingly good, exceedingly brave?
The good not always wins and the honest almost
always loses as if this were the counter-earth.

Watching the gentle trembling summer trees across
the surface of the lake where he studied the
distance to be traveled with his dark eyes, in
Michigan I see clocks that show nothing, for time
stops there. Hero who fights not only with hands
but with heart and mind: a holy hero whose name

as his soft voice moves the golden tresses of air,
swelling sounds of music. Thumps of hearts, rhythmic
speed of songs cover Mexico City, Haifa or those African
towns his eyes beheld. Paris, he loved and let his dark,
thinning hair flutter in the breeze there. Uncountable
crowns, prize of myriad thanks with every breath of
the living. Where he once used the sidewalks,
because he walked there, now paved with gold. We
walked the same streets of the blessed city, ate the
same bread, breathed the same air and witnessed the
same barbarism which is still with us. The dream of
mankind, of peace, shall not always be a dream.
At the new home of Muses where the pilgrimage of
poets proffering prayers and freshly minted songs
to be engraved in marble comes, from where he
started on his journey of scathless happiness
of a child, one bows his head low before the
greatness of a nation which gave him to us.

How long will last the marble? How long lasts bronze?
Greatest art and knowledge on earth is to consult
heaven about things to come. To wrest an answer
from heavenly powers and see something invisible
materialize. William Blake to see angels crouching
on a tree, the Prophet Ezekiel under green branches,
the soul of his brother leaving his body at the
moment of death and entering through the ceiling
in joy and clasping hands; to hear Milton, blind,
predicting the day of his own death: we hear sirens
of firetrucks, ambulances, noise of airplanes, racing
cars drowning out the music of chirping bird-songs
and our voices in the spring. Winds blow differently
in our time and the sun shines in a less encouraging
way, because, for many, ignorance still pays and the

vileness of man is still unchecked. But when one's life
or death can be so meaningful in its greatness and
consequences, the intent of terrorizing and enslaving
mankind cannot succeed. If everybody in every land
would kneel down and pray earnestly for a week,
peace, perhaps, could be restored on earth.

Sorting out the confusing state of dreams, horrors,
catastrophes that reach uppermost heaven, to see as
poets do also with spiritual eyes: no one can hide
anything nor can cover crime. We all live in the open.
Even the innermost thoughts of man are readable
by a simple out-of-body experience. Admiring the
flight of geese in the mirror of the sky: soul is
infinitely more precious than body. If persons would
know what is important and how important is something,
they would flock to learn it on earth. However,
behaviour overtakes most beings and drowns them.

It is not ours to say the earthly stay is long.
Not ours to see we wither away in wasting time.
It is true we die but yet we still live on. We live
on in colors of an invisible light. It is the affair
of humans to explore the world and create a better
one, even pre-empting future. Trees made out of
small lightnings, objects radiating light diffuse
brightness without shadows. The gold sand beaches
and windless horizons of eternity, blue isles in the
distance awaiting, - we are exiled for a few years
to earth. We are being held in abeyance here. A
garden where praise grows, prayers, where one catches
the triplicate self although the mirror does not
reflect views or persons. Not panicking over the return
when the air vibrates, in the palpitating peace we
penetrate rocks and go higher by turning more clean.

The world of thinking is tied somehow to words
and poets give proper emphasis to them. People
hardly realize the importance of this invisible world.
Aura of sanctity that envelopes a name, carrying the
sum-total of a person, sticks, as sawdust to honey.
World made out of pure songs, songs learned before birth
or taught by the beauty of ice-coated trees in front of
a sunset or colors of a spring behind a dusk: words,
songs celebrate an infinitely noble being, the globe
sings to praise one of its dearest souls. Subtleties of
hearts spread out as carpet so that everyone works on
weaving the world. Old people wait for the buds to open,
for swallows to take off from an antique vase. The world
stops for a moment. Who constantly work on themselves,
improving and bettering their hearts, souls, - poets try
to convey that not all lives are broken and not all
illusions shattered or lost. Messengers returned, the
aquamarine light of air, turquoise thoughts, Venetian
blue attachments and the azure loft of light, joy of
watching the steady stream of thoughts in vibrant shapes,
lights, colors: the air is light and in it we live.

Unlimited freedom is birthright of every human
on earth. Superabundance of oneself, spirit or soul
that cannot be annihilated or destroyed. Virtue for
virtue, memory of good deeds dictates our steps.
As in Budapest, in Stockholm the evening sky is still
full of yellow ribbons and in the mellowed late
December sunshine the wind orchestrates the unmusical
sounds of clattering chrysanthemums and brown oak leaves
rustling in the grass. A distinct feeling, deep within,
conveys Raoul Wallenberg is still alive, my
unmistakable conviction that he will never die.

COMMEDIA RUSSICA

MY HANGING REHEARSAL

We deny that it hurts to remember, for
it would reveal our vulnerability.
Our sufferings lift us above ourselves that
we may not break. But turning to the past
in hope of a solution is not quite correct
since we know our present will soon explode.
The unfinished history of Thucydides left
open the question whether the Sicilian
Expedition was a glorious victory or a
disastrous defeat. How immeasurably naive we
are in believing anything on earth can be
settled in a few years by words or arms.

When I opened the door I did not know what
was going to happen. I saw members of the
Defensive Authority of the State in the dim
light of the night. I was gagged with a
handkerchief before I could cry out and in a
flash three men ran into my small apartment.
They looked like brigands, members of a
robber-gang. Two from across the room and the
third quite near leveled their pistols at me
and one of them said:"Get your coat
and come with us. We are the Defensive
Authority of the State. Don't make any cry,
sign or superfluous movement, otherwise you'll
be shot like a dog. Understand?"- I nodded.
"Well, go", the man snarled with a pocked
face, signaling the way with his gun.

I felt at this moment like a little mouse finding
itself before a giant snake. My whole life, a
thousand things flitted through my brain. I knew
whoever leaves his home with the Defensive
Authority of the State, the famed Secret Police
of Hungary, the AVH, never returns, the family
never sees him again, - no one will know what
happened to him. At the very most, if he is
executed, they will send the hangman's bill to
his widow or children. I had heard the bill
was often so high that the family could only pay
by selling all their belongings.

In the car I sat between two secret agents
who pointed their guns at me. They warned
me before we started that if I dared to move,
I would be shot immediately. I didn't move.
I almost held my breath. Only my eyes
flashed from left to right and back, from one
gun to the other. I knew that as a curse of
civilization the stars can no longer be seen
over the cities at night. I could not see them
from the middle of the back seat. I watched
like one sentenced to death in a gas chamber
with increased thirst for life others, the
streets, shopwindows swimming in the light. I
looked at the sidewalkers, the worn-out faces,
sorrowful expressions. I knew them as I knew the
streets, the houses and trees: all dear to me.
I was thinking of father: he has started over
eleven times from scratch with mother because
of wars, revolutions, inflations and other
disasters. What will he think of me if I
disappear as most likely I will? We could hardly
make enough money for food, - I remember the
winter of 1946 when my sister and I ate only

bread dunked in oil. Occasionally we also had
salt and red pepper. Coffee never, nor tea, meat
or vegetables. Sometime we had molasses
as sugar. Once my tongue went white from hunger:
for four days there was nothing to eat. Silver
and gold can buy not a thing when there is
nothing to buy. A miracle was when onions were
smuggled to us through the Soviet soldiers'
line and potatoes once by our parents. This was
the winter when I saw our old house, now
occupied by the Minister of Transportation,
himself cutting my father's folio book with
a saw in the garden for the fireplace. He was
a streetcar driver before but now for 'services'
to the Party he, with his elementary schooling,
was elevated and declared 'honorary educated'.

After about a half an hour driving I saw with
increasing apprehension and fear, that we were going
directly toward the Kerepesi cemetery. One time
this cemetery lay far outside the city but because
of the progress and the population, it lies
just in the very heart of the capital. It was
rare to bury someone there. I guessed correctly
that was where we were going. The car stopped
for a moment before the gate. The driver blew
the horn as if in a code, the gate opened
and the car drove in. I was unsure of the way
from then on. I knew only that at the end of
the cemetery the car stopped and I was forced
out with such words that I can't repeat.
Then like raging sadists, the agents kicked me
at random with their muddy, naily boots. Despite
a fever, which I had had for some days, or
perhaps with the help of it, I succeeded staying
on my feet regardless of the kicks. I think

today it was my good fortune for if I had
fallen they would have kicked me to death.
When I staggered, they grabbed my shoulders,
my arms and thrust me some yards forward,
to the wall of the cemetery where
I observed a freshly dug grave.

"The enemies of the People's Democracy all have
this common place", - said the chief of the gang.
I did not hear any sound from the others. Then,
as if nothing in the world would have happened,
he added calmly and naturally these words: "We
have the order that you should be shot down like
a dog into this freshly dug grave. But we are men.
We will take the responsibility ourselves because
you are a religious man, and give you three minutes
to prepare yourself for death and make peace
with your God." And they stepped back a bit.

At that moment my life was meaningless to me.
I knew there was no way out. No thoughts came to
my mind. I looked at the stars which now I could
see and felt that among them God reigned, drying
the shower of my tears with his velvet hands.

I knew that the loss of one man's soul would
not raise hell or a word in the West.
Even the mass arrests going on in Hungary
would not bother the so-called intellectuals
and leaders of the West. What I did not know
though was that even the ten million strong
population of entire Hungary, or added to it the
fate of millions in Czechoslovakia, Bulgaria,

Romania, Poland means nothing to those free.
I could not have guessed that the fate of even
one billion enslaved human beings means absolutely
nothing and youth would just as well dance in
Western night-clubs as businessmen would sell their
souls and the bodies of their dead mothers for short
term profits. I should have guessed then that we were
all sold into slavery, that the many generations lying
in the graves had worked themselves to death for
the benefit and well-being of the West and now
the tyrants of the East. If someone dares to
immolate himself in the streets of Budapest or
Prague, university students in the West will all
just laugh rather than demand actions from their own
governments. When half of the world is sold out
thus... They live on a volcano and do not notice.

Then the weight of my overburdened heart was taken
away by God. I felt a lion's force in my sick and
tortured body. I knew beyond the stars there are
no more tears, crying, suffering, neither the
Defensive Authority of the State nor Russian
occupation and diabolical marxism.

"Are you ready?"- a question like a whip
clove the air. "Yes." "May we shoot?"- "Yes", -
I answered again. But they didn't shoot.
"What a nice game", - said the chief to the
others and they broke out in mad guffaws.
Human hyenas, unstopping and unstoppable
laughter. After long minutes when they had
laughed themselves out at the successful joke',
they asked me politely to take a seat in the
car again because the 'serious' part of
things would only follow later.

For the first time in my life I asked God
to take away my life and not permit me to suffer
any longer. This Russian comedy was a real
Hungarian tragedy for me. And when the car
started to roll again I thought of those
hundreds and thousands of political prisoners
who had been arrested before me and those who
would be arrested in days to come and I sighed
bitterly from an infinitely heavy heart.

I did not know how I felt. I still do not
know whether it was shame, fear or humility.
The one who was driving dealt a blow to my
kidney and now it was aching terribly.
One of the fingers on my left hand had been
kicked out of joint. I also had a great headache.
I kept looking straight ahead where we were
going. Still many people were in the streets.
Electric cars rumbling. On Octagon Square
the mechanical news was running as usual.
Everything familiar, everything normal. I
thought I observe everything from another dimension.
We crossed the Margaret Bridge and turned into
the Fö utca Prison. There I was asked, again
very politely, to walk across the courtyard
where a small lamp lighted a door.

I did. But when I arrived at the courtyard's
center, about six or seven watchdogs ran toward
me, barking mad. I was expecting them to jump
on me, but only one of them attacked and bit
my left leg. Then the dogs were withdrawn with
a whistle and I started again slowly, toward the
lighted door. Except the lamp, everything was black.

As tourists who have seen a country just before
a military take-over and can never go back to it,
I felt the outside world has been lost for me.
When we cannot get accustomed to a certain treatment,
we must stand it, accept and cope with it.
I was close to understand those who could so
easily forget laws, morals and commit crimes:
bandits of the soul. We extinguish ourselves.

I was taken to a lower basement room where there
were heavy plush curtains but no windows.
Some were standing around in blue uniforms of
the secret police. There were also two soldiers.
An officer seated behind a large desk. He asked:
"What are you here for?" -"I don't know, I wasn't
told", - I said."Liar", - shouted a soldier and ran
towards me from the left. "Liar", - rattled from
his throat and he kicked my kidney again, the
same kidney. I fainted.

After being splashed with a pail of water I
regained consciousness. The officer explained
the soldiers were there in order to avenge any
kind of aggressive or impertinent answers, and
I was told to abstain from unfamiliar words.
The he repeated: "So you don't know why are
you here?" - "I don't", - I said. "Well", - he
answered, - "if your memory is short then I'll
refresh it". He bowed his head in the papers
and read slowly: "Treason, continual spying
for a foreign power, reactionary attitude,
pacifist humanism... Is that enough?"

"Enough", - I said. "Then it will be better
if you tell us everything", - and he looked
at me with his eagle-eyes. "If you will make
a confession, we will take it as an extenuating
circumstance". "Yes", - I said, - "but I don't
know what should I confess to". "Liar", - shouted
the soldier again and he pounded my head with
his fists. The other soldier pushed me down
with his gun. My nose started to bleed when they
kicked out some of my teeth and I fainted again.

When I was washed up they served me coffee and
I received first aid. They asked my opinion about
movie-stars, soccer games, about operas and the
weather. They asked me if I was hungry. They were
so extremely polite I had the impression that a
beast rose up in them once every hour and they
lost their minds. The questioning started again.

At that time I was translating Swinburne's drama
Atalanta in Calydon into Hungarian and the most
I could imagine I did against my own country was
to consult some books in English in a library.
If one's not paranoid here must be crazy, I
thought, and tried to listen with eddying ears
to inside voices. I thought the giants of spirit
would rise and demonstrate against this injustice.
Once with closed eyes I was able to see God
in a vision. In my underground cell mornings
came without the blue fragrance of red roses and
I did not know there were mornings. But if they
came they arrived as bulldozers cleaning away
the ruins of my dreams. To me the sky was on its
knees there. In delirium I heard the constant

chit-chats of a sea. I was throwing up my soul
as the horrid ocean throws up bodies. In my country
one cannot even laugh free. The gaoler was himself
the gangish Khan, with sadistic features.

Once I was summoned again from my cell for another
questioning. I was taken up to the third basement
floor. With my guardian-gaolers I entered a large
room. I was expecting to see the eagle-eyed man
but he wasn't there. Behind a desk a tall man was
standing with always turning eyes. Two other men
in civilian clothes were beside him. When I stopped
in front of him with the guardsmen, he grasped a
paper on the desk and without asking who I was, read:
"In the name of the Hungarian People's Republic!
The Court, after establishing the fact that you
committed the most serious crimes against the nation,
treason as well as spying for a foreign power,
has found you guilty of these crimes. As an
aggravating circumstance we took your obstinate
denial. According to the procedure and the written
proofs, there is no doubt that you committed your
crimes against the working classes and against
the Socialist Camp. Therefore, on the basis of the
Criminal Laws, article such and such, paragraph
so and so, you are sentenced to death by hanging.
The judgment comes to force immediately and there
is no appeal. The judgment shall be executed
at once". Then he looked up from his paper.
Glancing at me he said: "Executioner, do your duty!"
Only then did I turn to my right where, in the
corner of the room, there was a gallows and an
executioner with two assistants. They were in

under-shirts. I turned back to the officer.
His face was ice-cold, impassive and he asked
his assistants at the desk: "Who is next?"

I did not hear the answer. My hands were tied
by the executioner's assistants and I had seen
that in the other end of the room there were
about six or seven corpses, covered with brown
paper. I saw only the shoes. As if I had heard
that nine more were to be executed that day.
Blindfolded I was, ordered to stand on a stool
with a rope around my neck. The officer said again:
"Do you want to avail yourself of the privilege of
the last word? It won't make much difference but
if you make a confession, you could relieve yourself
a bit". "I have nothing to say", - I answered.

I smelled the smoke of a cigarette and felt the
tightening of the rope around my neck. I had to
stand on tiptoe. Then the footstool was kicked
out from under me. And I fell down to the concrete
floor with the rope around my neck. They took away
the blindfold. The executioner, assistants, the
officer, the civilians, the guards broke into
mad guffaws. They were guffawing with their bellies.

I was still lying on the floor with the rope on me.
I thought of Florence's beautiful church, the white
Santa Croce, and the fake tombs and epitaphs there
hiding the memory of some creative giants that
we never should know where and why they rest.
Uncreative violence: I thought even the corpses

here were fake and I was the target of a demonic
ploy. Irreverence, scurrility and vilification,
abuse were heaped on me. Between East and West
the spirit is the loser, since neither powers
care about it. There are people in the West
who are mercilessly free and would rather feed
a single cat and see ten adults die by hunger than
move a finger to do something about the world
they live in. There are politicians who lie and
promise New Jerusalems and miracles to their
constituents, but care nothing for another race.

The soul has no shape, one thinks, but wrong is he.
Light-years of non-existence ride over the dreams.
And we all turn back as Orpheus to see the
better half of us.
                        I was drawn back. The
officer said: "It must be recognized you were
very brave. Hope you will be as courageous
at the real hanging as you were today!"

SLAPDASH   POEM

Square-headed men
co-occurence   gannetry
chough side-slipping down the wind
solemnitized and teased
leonazed and gazed
bugainvillea on the bungalows
surfeited eyes with castanets
surf - noisy coast
here died the bravest   gallows
fair-haired stars combing
gloomy mood   looping dresses
the bride wore clothes
Strong Quartet. Adagio mafioso
summersaulting carpetbraggers
soaprano

rox

SIGNATURES

I signed my name in my wife's dream as
Paulinus the poet and she wrote down hers as
Elizabeth B.Browning in another dream of hers.
The fire of songs still escorts.
Songs ablooming, fire of eyes and hearts,
the soul. Love is a great load to carry
even on the winged sandals of Perseus.

People in the sky, angels feel a
commitment towards the living and want
to help, patronize and care.
Drinking the empyrean, asking God on knees:
why do lovers make such tremendous efforts
to stabilize time and futurize present?

Throwing one on the waves of music,
caressed by eyes, kissed by thoughts, poets
sow dreams and let emotions grow, bloom, ripen.

Bravery seldom begins at home and never
ends there. Who goes out and seizes life, wades
through the ecstasies of grief, completing
the conquest of the masterpieces of art...

Plunging through body as across a white hole
into another realm from which it is unwise
to return to earth...
Illusions of the material universe trailing,
a life intermingled with dreams, butterflies
in teams... Kissed my hand!
The purest times are still to come.

THE TREES TALKED

The trees talked to me and said: "Don't try
to live quickly. Take time. Submit yourself
to the seasons. Observe and embrace us sometimes.
You can't buy time. So live with it. Live slow."

The stones talked to me and said: "Be firm.
Do not run, don't move or change. Be of one kind.
Be the foundation of the earth, the law."
And the air talked to me and said: "Be soft."

The flowers talked to me then and I listened:
"Be unique and delicate in your actions
and in your words. They are the fragrance
which flies around you and away to others."

The clouds talked to me and said: "Be above all."
The rivers whispered and gurgled: "Don't listen
to men. Take a dip in yourself." The birds
told me: "Sing." And the sun said: "Shine."

The sunset talked saying: "Be overwhelming."
The sunrise said to me: "Open yourself up."
The night came and the earth said: "Stay. Dream."
A new day strolled in and heaven said: "Come on."

And I listened and accepted all advice
and lived according to the rules of nature,
asked my fellow men to follow and they laughed
and said: "You're crazy. You have lost your mind."

ANTI-FEBRUARY SONG

The winter is too long.
My spirits are low
and I just dread along
in the slushy snow.

The sun never shines.
Patience is worn out.
Hopes unexploded mines:
am voicing them aloud.

Rains that pulled the fall,
autumn that pull'd the rains
are well behind us all
except the bleak terrains.

Oblivion has no limits.
Steam bridges of light
and the roses of spirits
are dark, frost-applied.

The misery is enhanced,
enlarged are the pains.
The birds fly high against
the incoming planes.

MEXICAN IDYLL

Carved on the temple stones in the jungle
crocodile priestesses and jaguar priests
with bloody knives. Furious gleaming of
insects, strange, frightened cries of birds.
Tumbled stairs led to more tumbled stairs.
The past was relieved in part when night came
to the small Mexican town. Carrying lighted
candles in hand, chanting in muffled voice,
the whole population crossed the large
square in front of the church on knees.

PEOPLE OF THE DREAMS

People of the dreams know me well as might:
they talk to me and listen when I talk.
For vacationing go we there by night
but in our world they never take a walk.

Our music is made by roars of guns,
sirens, clattering gadgets, a train or bus.
We have made ourselves aliens, orphans
and our hope lies ahead of us.

People of the dreams tell me otherwise.
We lost future, they tell in unison.
Dream of mankind is still a compromise:
salvation by Jesus, the son of the sun.

COLLECTOR'S GUIDE TO DREAMS

Traveling through space and seeing places,
- what the soul does when it is free, -
traveling outside of time and beyond memory
as in a myth, you may want to remember
pink bamboo orchids in girls' black hair,
the blazing red lilies and pallid asphodels
under a narrow coombe. You want to remember
and keep them all.

After the gods abandoned Olympus the peaks
remained, capped by cloud-coifs, -
wisps of mist clinging to fake castles, -
and the immense view of life and death was
revealed from the valleys below fetlock-deep
in clover and all the flowers blooming
at the end of April or
beginning of May.

One more afternoon squeezed from life,
one more winter, one more hope: melancholy
of a twilight at Delphi where the Doric
columns sunbathed in silence and sward of
flowers climbed the slope, vandyked hem swinging
at the knees by the touch of huge paniers of
lobelia: you would keep them all.

Un-licensed poet who somehow earned the
degree of Master of Hope, you would remember
and preserve kiss-castles, the toffee-flavored
smell of lonely weekends and worrisome
holidays, halls created from crystals,

pears out of pure gold. Not that it would
matter, since these were your dreams along
with animals that talk, flowers that fly
and sing. Dawns coming from inside, we
migrate with the ducks.

It seemed these were all illusions,
though the vividness and exuberance of
experience compelled you to obey the effects of
pictures just as when you get lost at an art-show
and there is no way out unless you fight. Voices
coming alive in transparent shapes, smiling, and
you attach a label to them, to the landscape
the sun that sticks.

Emerald-flashing rivers, lawns curled up to
the horizon, arrangement of bushes with stars
in Christmas-fashion, lights in hordes, parading
through lace-towers of invisible drizzles.
You lunch with the Queen of Fairies.
That's what you want to keep.

Nothing from earth, whatsoever.
Moral torture of the West ignored, sidestepped,
forgiven the entire lewd, eroticized society
where for a big decency display you still
turn to very small towns.

One who was strong for too long a time
and now uncontrollably cries: so much
sorrow that it breaks the sky.
Visible is not an aid to the unseen,
and dreams are not walking canes.

Picking words, daisies by a small child,
flowers still bloom which are not here.
The gold Mohar tree blossoming, immense
roses, dapple-eared lilies and
caruscating hollyhocks. A spring comes
forth from the heart, a foaming gulf
rushing toward a meadow where fountain pens
were planted and are now in buds. Rainbows
twisted, knotted, chained and handcuffed
to mother-of-pearl banks.

Buried between lips I feel myself on fire
and know my love escapes from me. My shadow
as red horses flying without wings, sneaks
up to melt with yours in flames.

DON'T DARE EVEN TO SIGH

Subhuman beings and supercrooks
punch you on the nose daily
to learn humility.

The overmighty gallop across
the graves in pursuit of
personal gain.

Learn to live with slights,
snubs, offenses.
Don't dare even to sigh.

F I R E W O R K S

Exploding daffodils.
Niagaring fire-snakes.
Giant blue hortensia, larkspur and pansy-
    halos blooming around the
    Statue of Liberty: the stars
    spill through her fingers and
    twinkle down to the sea.
Electric lilies and birds with
    wings on fire, pulling
    long lighted trails.
Crowning all the Greek fire of the
    sky setting the water ablaze,
    enveloping the melting stars
    in pink gossamer.